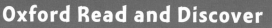

Oxford Read and Discover

Discover! **6**

Caring For Our Planet

Joyce Hannam

Contents

OXFORD
UNIVERSITY PRESS

OXFORD
UNIVERSITY PRESS

Great Clarendon Street, Oxford OX2 6DP

Oxford University Press is a department of the University of Oxford. It furthers the University's objective of excellence in research, scholarship, and education by publishing worldwide in

Oxford New York

Auckland Cape Town Dar es Salaam Hong Kong Karachi Kuala Lumpur Madrid Melbourne Mexico City Nairobi New Delhi Shanghai Taipei Toronto

With offices in

Argentina Austria Brazil Chile Czech Republic France Greece Guatemala Hungary Italy Japan Poland Portugal Singapore South Korea Switzerland Thailand Turkey Ukraine Vietnam

OXFORD and OXFORD ENGLISH are registered trade marks of Oxford University Press in the UK and in certain other countries

© Oxford University Press 2010

The moral rights of the author have been asserted

Database right Oxford University Press (maker)

First published 2010
2014 2013
10 9 8 7 6

No unauthorized photocopying

ISBN: 978 0 19 464559 1

An Audio CD Pack containing this book and a CD is also available, ISBN 978 0 19 464599 7

The CD has a choice of American and British English recordings of the complete text.

An accompanying Activity Book is also available, ISBN 978 0 19 464569 0

Printed in China

This book is printed on paper from certified and well-managed sourcesa.

ACKNOWLEDGEMENTS

Illustrations by: Kelly Kennedy pp.16, 21, 25; Dusan Pavlic/Beehive Illustration p.36; Alan Rowe p.36; Mark Ruffle pp.8, 24, 38, 46.

The Publishers would also like to thank the following for their kind permission to reproduce photographs and other copyright material: Alamy pp.5 (Picture Contact), 7 (Wayne Hutchinson), 9 (Helga Lutz/flood), 14 (K-Photos/wind farm), 15 (John Hensall), 17 (Johnny Greig Travel Photography), 20 (David Ball), 22 (Stuart Kelly), 23 (Floralpik/compost bin), 27 (Edward Parker), 28 (Frans Lemmens), 31 (Mike Hill), 33 (Photoshot Holdings Ltd); Getty Images pp.4 (Carl Warner), 10 (Torsten Blackwood/AFP), 13 (Felipe Rodriguez Fernandez/Photographer's Choice/solar power station), 14 (Robert Francis/Robert Harding World Imagery/Svartsengi), 25 (Rob and Ann Simpson/Visuals Unlimited/periwinkle), 34 (Julian Sullivan); Robert Gilhooly p.23 (Kamikatsu recycling); Oxford University Press pp.3, 6, 16, 18, 25 (olive oil), 26, 29, 30, 35; PA Photos p.19 (AP/QiinetiQ.com/Press Association Images); Practical Action pp.9 (floating garden), 11 (high house); Still Pictures pp.12 (Fred Dott,Hamburg/Argus-foto), 13 (Mark Edwards/solar cooker), 21 (RESMI SENAN-UNEP), 32 (Nigel Dickinson).

With thanks to Ann Fullick for science checking

Introduction

On our planet Earth there are many beautiful places. Sadly, some of the things that people do are damaging our planet. We must care for it, to keep it safe and clean for all the plants, animals, and people living here.

What beautiful places can you see below?
What beautiful places are there in your country?
How do people damage our planet?
How can we care for our planet?

Now read and discover more about caring for our beautiful planet!

Using Resources Carefully

Our planet gives us many natural resources like air to breathe and water to drink. It gives us plants and animals to eat, and coal and oil to make electricity. We need to use all these resources carefully.

Some of Earth's Natural Resources

Renewable Resources

Some natural resources, like water, sun, wind, soil, animals, and plants, can replace themselves naturally. They are called renewable resources. They will not run out if we don't use them too quickly. If we use them carefully, we will have lots of these resources to use for a long time.

We All Need Water

Water is one of the most important natural resources on Earth. We need fresh water to drink, and we need it to grow and cook food, and to wash. Plants, animals, and people all need water to live.

About 70% of Earth is covered with water, but most of this water is salt water in oceans. People need fresh water to drink, but only about 3% of Earth's water is fresh water.

In some countries there isn't enough water. Sometimes, people have to travel a long way to collect water, or they move to a new place where there is water.

Collecting Water

Non-Renewable Resources

We use fossil fuels like coal, gas, and oil in power stations to make electricity. We use electricity to power lights. Refrigerators, televisions, and computers all need electricity, too. Many people use electricity to cook and to heat their homes. We also use electricity to power some vehicles, and we use oil to make gasoline to power cars and other vehicles.

The problem is that these fossil fuels cannot be replaced, so when we have used them all, they will run out. They are called non-renewable resources, and we are using them too quickly.

Discover!

In 2007, the four countries that used the most electricity were the USA, China, Russia, and Japan. Countries with more people need more electricity.

Using Electricity

Pollution

Sometimes we make our resources dirty. This is called pollution. We pollute the air when we use fossil fuels to make energy like electricity. We pollute water when we put waste into it. People, animals, and plants all need clean air and water.

What Can We Do?

There are lots of ways we can help. We must keep water clean, and we must not waste it. Some charities are helping people to collect and store water. They are also building new dams, wells, and pumps, so that people can have clean water nearer their homes.

We must use non-renewable resources carefully, and we must not waste them. Scientists are investigating ways to use renewable resources, like sun, wind, and water, to make electricity so that we don't need to use so many fossil fuels. We can also try to use less electricity.

A New Water Pump

→ Go to pages 36–37 for activities.

#
Keeping Our Planet Cool

Scientists think that Earth's climate is changing and the weather is getting more extreme. They think that this is happening because Earth is getting warmer. Why is this happening, and how can we keep our planet cool?

The Greenhouse Effect

Earth gets heat from the sun. Some of the heat escapes into space, but some is trapped by a blanket of gases. This keeps Earth warm enough for us to live here, and it's called the greenhouse effect because it works like a greenhouse.

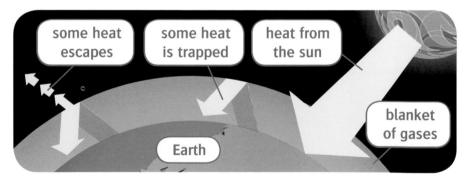

some heat escapes

some heat is trapped

heat from the sun

blanket of gases

Earth

Global Warming

When we use fossil fuels we make a gas called carbon dioxide. Scientists think that we are putting too much carbon dioxide into the air. The carbon dioxide increases the greenhouse effect and Earth gets warmer. This is called global warming.

Extreme Weather

Scientists think that global warming is changing our climate and making the weather more extreme. This is a problem for people, animals, and plants.

Hurricanes are getting more dangerous. In 2005, a huge hurricane hit New Orleans in the USA. About 2,000 people died, and most of the city was flooded.

There are many rivers in Bangladesh. There are always floods in the rainy season, but the floods are getting worse. Every year, some people die and thousands of people lose their homes.

Discover!

In Bangladesh, some people make floating gardens. They grow food on them, so that they have food during the floods.

9

In the Sahara Desert in Africa, there is not enough rain and the desert is getting bigger. People have left their homes because they can't grow food. The Gobi Desert in China and Mongolia is also getting bigger. Desert sand blows all the way into cities in North Korea and South Korea.

Melting Ice

Earth is getting warmer and the ice is melting at the North and South Poles. As this ice changes to water, the sea level is getting higher. This is dangerous for low countries like Bangladesh, and for low islands.

Tuvalu is a country in the Pacific Ocean and it's made of groups of islands. Parts of the capital, Funafati, are now only 10 centimeters above sea level. Scientists think that the ocean will soon cover the land, and the people who live there will have to move to other countries like New Zealand or Australia.

Funafati, Tuvalu

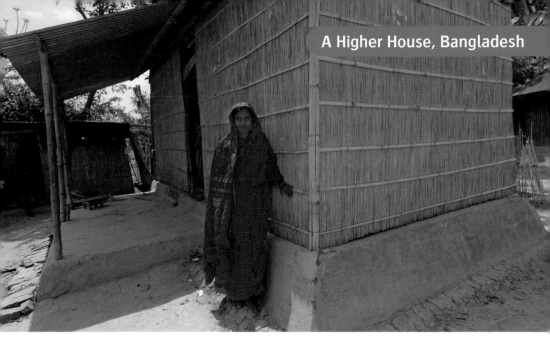
A Higher House, Bangladesh

What Can We Do?

Scientists are investigating ways of predicting extreme weather so that people can be ready for it. Charities are working with people to build stronger and higher homes. They are also giving people special radios so that they can hear about extreme weather and move to a safer place.

Our planet has natural ways to reduce carbon dioxide. Oceans and plants use carbon dioxide, so we must protect our oceans and plants.

We must try to keep Earth cool by using fewer fossil fuels and producing less carbon dioxide. We need electricity, but we can make it without using fossil fuels. Instead, we can use nuclear energy, or natural energy from the sun, wind, or water.

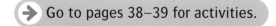 Go to pages 38–39 for activities.

Making Clean Electricity

Scientists are investigating ways of making clean electricity that is not made with fossil fuels. This is important if we want to reduce global warming and pollution. How is electricity made in your country?

Nuclear Energy

Nuclear power stations make electricity without using fossil fuels. They don't put carbon dioxide into the air, but they produce dangerous radioactive waste. This waste is put underground or under the ocean, where it must stay for thousands of years before it's safe.

If there's an accident at a nuclear power station, dangerous radioactive waste can get into the air and travel a long way. In 1986 an accident happened in Chernobyl in Ukraine. People died and many more people were sick. About 336,000 people had to move away to new homes. Scientists are working hard to make nuclear power stations safer.

A Nuclear Power Station, France

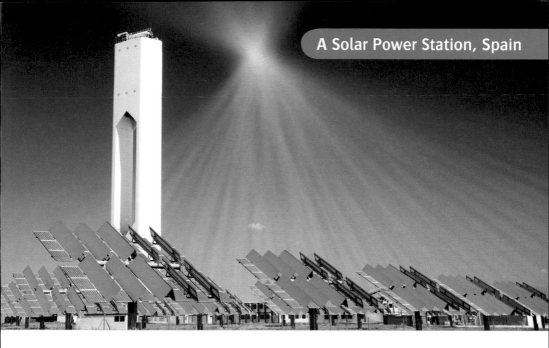

Solar Energy

Another way to make electricity is to use the heat from the sun. Solar power stations only work well in places where it's very sunny all year long.

In many countries, people use solar energy from solar panels to heat water in homes, offices, and swimming pools, and to power watches, calculators, and road signs.

Discover! In sunny countries, you can cook by using only heat from the sun. All you need is sunshine and a solar panel!

13

Wind Energy

Wind turbines use the energy from the wind to make electricity. We can build wind turbines in isolated places and also in the oceans. They can be useful in colder countries where there is not enough sunshine to use solar energy to make electricity. Germany, for

Wind Turbines, USA

example, makes 6% of its electricity in wind farms. All around the world there are more and more wind farms.

Geothermal Energy

Geothermal energy comes from the heat that is trapped underground. Hot water and steam from underground can be used to heat buildings, and to make electricity. In Iceland there is lots of hot water underground. Geothermal power stations make about 25% of Iceland's electricity.

Discover!

Hot water from the Svartsengi geothermal power station in Iceland is used to fill an outdoor pool. It's clean enough for swimming.

Energy From Water

We can make electricity by using energy from moving water in rivers, lakes, or oceans. This is called hydroelectricity. The first hydroelectric power station was built in 1882. It was a simple water wheel. It made enough electricity for 250 light bulbs.

The biggest hydroelectric power station in the world today is the Three Gorges Dam in China. It can make enough electricity for whole cities!

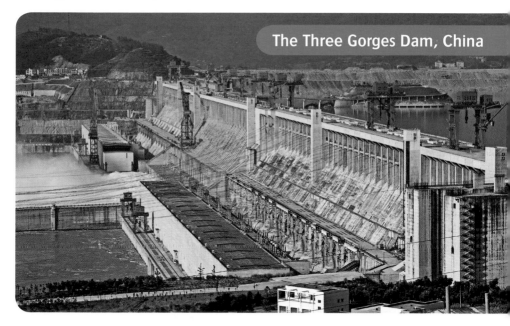

The Three Gorges Dam, China

In 1966, scientists in France started to make electricity using energy from ocean tides. Then other scientists used energy from waves. Scientists are now investigating better ways of using energy from tides and waves to make cheap and clean electricity.

→ Go to pages 40–41 for activities.

4 Reducing Travel

Most of us travel to school or to work every day. Maybe we travel by car to go shopping or to visit friends, or by plane to go on vacation. Why should we travel less?

The Problem with Travel

Cars, planes, buses, and ships all put carbon dioxide into the air. This increases the greenhouse effect and makes our planet warmer. Vehicles also pollute the air with other gases. This makes our cities dirty.

Discover!

Airports are getting very, very busy. About 59,000 international passengers travel through the main airport in New York every day.

What Can We Do?

It's very difficult to stop traveling, but we can think carefully about the way we travel. For short journeys, we can walk or cycle. This is also better than sitting in a car because exercise is good for us. We can share cars or use public transportation for some journeys. We can try to use small cars because they use less fuel than big ones.

We should also reduce the number of vehicles that we make, because we use fossil fuels to power the factories where we make the vehicles.

Some people try to fly less often, and if they have to fly, they do something called carbon offsetting. They find out how much carbon dioxide their journey will produce. Then they pay to plant enough trees to use all the carbon dioxide that the journey made.

A Solar-Powered Car

Cleaner Cars

Engineers are investigating how to make car engines cleaner so that they won't damage our planet so much. Modern cars have machines called catalytic converters that change exhaust gases into cleaner gases.

Instead of using gasoline, some cars use electricity and others use a mixture of gasoline and electricity. Some cars use fuels made from plants. These biofuels can be made from nuts, corn, and other plants. There are also a few cars that use electricity made from solar energy. Maybe in the future all cars will be powered in these ways.

Cleaner Planes

Engineers are trying to make plane engines that don't pollute the air, but it's very difficult. They know that lighter planes with bigger wings use less fuel. They are designing better planes all the time.

Some planes can fly using biofuels, but many people think it's wrong to grow plants for planes. They say that we need the land to grow food for people. What do you think?

A few planes are already powered by solar energy, but they don't have any space for passengers.

Discover!

The *Zephyr* plane is powered by solar energy. It's very light and it doesn't carry people. In 2008 it flew without stopping for 83 hours!

Go to pages 42–43 for activities.

Keeping Our Planet Clean

Every day we throw away waste from our homes, schools, offices, and factories. This waste is collected in trucks, then some is recycled, and some is burned or put underground. What do you do with your waste?

Too Much Waste

People throw away too much waste. In some countries, there is not enough space to put any more waste underground. Some things that we throw away, like plastic bags, refrigerators, and cars, will stay underground for hundreds of years.

In the USA every person produces more than 2 kilograms of waste every day. So for the whole country that's more than 232 million metric tons!

Waste Makes Pollution

Sometimes, people throw waste into rivers, lakes, or the ocean. Human waste and waste from factories also pollute water. More than a billion people in the world do not have clean water to drink. Every day, people die from dirty drinking water.

Some people leave waste on streets, in the countryside, and on beaches. This pollutes our planet, and it's dangerous for animals if they eat the waste.

Deer Eating Waste

Too Many Plastic Bags

We throw away more plastic bags than anything else!
Plastic bags are a huge problem for our planet. It's
difficult to recycle them. You can use a plastic bag
for only five minutes, but it can take 500 years to
decompose. People throw away too many plastic bags
and this pollutes our cities, countryside, and oceans.
Many fish, birds, and other animals die if they eat a
plastic bag, because then they can't breathe or eat food.

If people have to pay for plastic bags, they will use
them less. In 2002, when people in Ireland were
asked to pay for plastic bags, the number of bags
used reduced by 90% in one year! In many countries
today, there are no free plastic bags.

Try to use plastic bags lots of times, or use a bag that
is made of a natural material instead.

What Can We Do?

When we throw things away we must do it carefully – never throw waste into streets, rivers, or the ocean.

We can throw away less waste, for example, we can reuse more things before we throw them away. We can throw away much less food and garden waste by using a compost bin. In a compost bin, worms and bacteria eat the waste and change it into good soil called compost. We can use compost to help plants to grow better.

Inside a Compost Bin

compost

Another way to reduce waste is to recycle things. Many people already recycle lots of things, like paper, cans, plastic and glass containers, and clothes. We can also recycle bigger things like parts of cars. The recycled materials can then be used again to make new things.

Discover!

In Kamikatsu in Japan, people are hoping to recycle everything by 2020. They divide their waste into 34 different types for recycling.

→ Go to pages 44–45 for activities.

23

6 Protecting Plants

Without plants, we would have nothing to eat. We also use plants to make clothes, homes, and medicines. Plants take carbon dioxide from the air, and they give us oxygen to breathe, too. Plants are really important!

Food Chains

All living things are part of food chains. Plants are at the start of all food chains because plants only need sunlight, water, and carbon dioxide from the air to make their food. Animals need to eat plants, or they eat other animals that eat plants. So we all need plants!

Four Food Chains

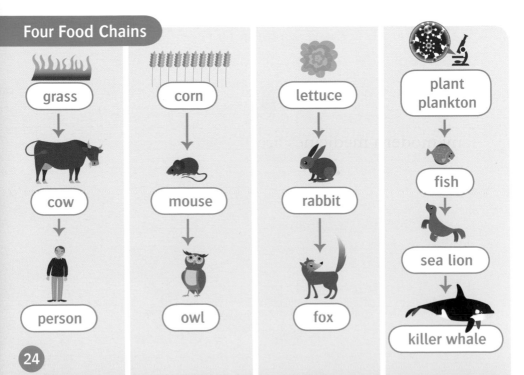

grass → cow → person

corn → mouse → owl

lettuce → rabbit → fox

plant plankton → fish → sea lion → killer whale

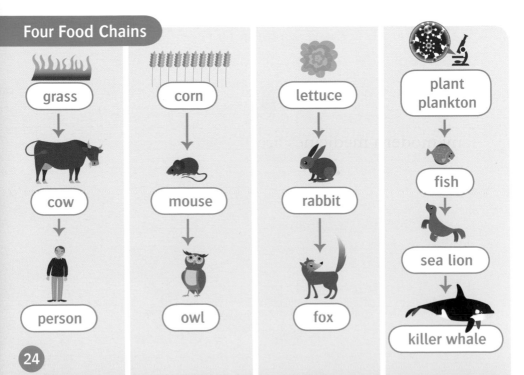

24

Food and Drink

Plants give us food like fruit, vegetables, and rice. We eat fruit and vegetables because they contain vitamins that keep us healthy. Cereal crops, like wheat and corn, give us flour to make bread. Many drinks, like tea, coffee, and chocolate come from plants. We also use some plants as herbs or spices to make our food taste good.

Discover!

We use olive trees in many ways. We can eat the fruit, and use oil made from the fruit for cooking. The oil is also good for our hair and skin.

Medicines

For thousands of years, people have used plants as medicines. Many modern medicines are made from chemicals that were first found in plants. Many plants that are used for medicines grow in rainforests. For example, the rosy periwinkle from Madagascar contains chemicals that can treat two types of cancer.

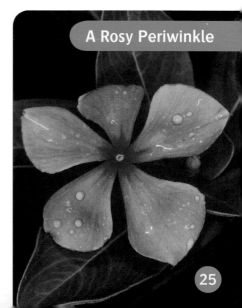

A Rosy Periwinkle

Reducing Global Warming

In the daytime, plants take carbon dioxide from the air to make their food. This helps to reduce global warming. It's one of our planet's natural ways to reduce carbon dioxide.

Plants in Danger

Plants need clean air and water to grow – polluted air and water can damage them. Global warming is also a problem. Some plants cannot grow in their usual place if the temperature gets too high, or if there is extreme weather like floods.

We are using too many trees. Big international companies cut down huge numbers of trees for wood to make furniture or paper. Sometimes they cut down trees in rainforests to make space to grow crops or to raise cattle, so that they can produce cheap food like palm oil and hamburgers.

People Cut Down Too Many Trees

Planting New Trees in the Amazon

What Can We Do?

If we keep our planet clean and use fewer fossil fuels to reduce global warming, we will save millions of plants.

We must also use fewer trees. We can use less paper and recycle it. Some charities collect money to buy trees to keep them safe. We can pay people to care for trees and use them in different ways to make money. For example, farmers can sell nuts from their trees. We must stop companies destroying rainforests to bring us cheap food.

We can plant new trees. Countries and big companies can also replace the trees that they use. Finland and Canada already do this.

➜ Go to pages 46–47 for activities.

Protecting Animals

Earth is home to many amazing animals, from tiny bacteria that we can't even see, to huge whales. We share our planet with all these other animals. Animals help us in many different ways and we must protect them.

We Need Animals

Many animals, like cows, sheep, and chickens, are raised for food. Farmers raise them to give us meat, cheese, eggs, and milk. In the ocean, there are fish farms where large numbers of fish are raised for food. We use animals to give us leather, wool, and feathers. Around the world, animals are also used to help us with work. They carry people and crops, and they help with farm work.

Getting Milk from a Goat

Collecting Honey from Bees

Useful Minibeasts

Insects, like beetles, flies, and ants, help the planet, too. Some insects carry pollen from flower to flower. Many flowers need pollen from another flower to make seeds. Bees fly from flower to flower to get nectar to make honey. People collect the honey and enjoy eating it! Many insects are useful because they eat waste, and worms help us by making compost and keeping the soil healthy.

Animals in Danger

Every animal has a special place to live called its habitat, but people are destroying many of these important habitats. When we cut down the rainforest trees, we destroy the habitat of gorillas and tigers, and hundreds of smaller animals. Global warming is also a problem for animals. For example, if too much ice at the North Pole melts, polar bears will lose their habitat.

Hunters kill some animals for money. Many elephants were hunted because people could sell their ivory tusks for a lot of money. Now this has stopped, but all around the world, hundreds of different types of animal, from insects to tigers, are disappearing because of lost habitats or hunting. Pollution is also a huge problem for animals.

What Can We Do?

We must protect habitats, and we must keep the countryside clean. Many countries have made special places called national parks or wildlife parks where wild animals can live safe from hunters. In Africa there are also safari parks where tourists from all around the world can come and see the animals in their natural habitat.

Elephants in a Safari Park in Kenya, Africa

Zoos Today

Many wild animals are kept in zoos or animal reserves. If they are rare animals, the last ones can be kept safe there. They can have babies and there will be more of them again. Many modern zoos keep animals in places similar to their natural habitat. Sometimes they take the animals back to their natural home when it's safe.

Some charities work to save rare animals and their habitats. You can pay to adopt an animal and help to keep it safe. These giant pandas live in a special animal reserve in China. Many people are adopting giant pandas and helping them here.

Giant Pandas in Woolong Reserve, China

Go to pages 48–49 for activities.

8 The Way Forward

Most people understand that we must care for our planet. We must now learn how to do it better. Earth is our home and we must protect it for the future. What will you do to care for our planet?

A Simple Life?

Some people think that modern city life is bad for Earth. We use too much energy and we make too much waste. They think that we should live in small villages, grow our own food on the land, and not travel far. This life would not damage our planet.

A Small Village, the Philippines

New Technology

Other people think that we cannot go back to a simpler way of living. They think that new technology can help us to find new, clean ways to travel and make energy.

You can see some of this new technology in new types of house design. These new houses don't use any energy from fossil fuels, but they are still comfortable in very hot or cold weather. They have solar panels in the roof, and they are made of wood from forests where trees are always replaced.

Do you think we should live more simply or use new technology? Or should we do both?

What Can We Do?

When we go shopping, we must think carefully about what we buy. Some food that we buy comes from near our homes. Other food comes on planes and ships from far away, and we use fossil fuels to transport it. Some people say we should eat more food that is grown near to our homes. Do we need summer fruit in winter? How much of the food that you buy was grown near where you live?

We must not be greedy. For example, no one wants oceans with no fish in them. We can take some fish, but we must not take too many. We must be careful not to use too many of Earth's natural resources too quickly.

In our everyday life we can all help the planet in small ways. We can reuse and recycle as much as possible to reduce waste and pollution. We can turn off lights to save electricity, and we can try not to use our cars too much, to reduce carbon dioxide. We can give money to charities that care for the planet. If millions of people do small things, this will make a difference.

It's Our Planet

Scientists think that we don't have much time to reduce global warming. So we have to change the way we live now. The people of Tuvalu and Bangladesh are worried about their future. So are the people near the Sahara and Gobi Deserts. They need everyone to help. We must all help to care for our planet.

→ Go to pages 50–51 for activities.

1 Using Resources Carefully

← Read pages 4–7.

1 **Write the words. Then write ✓ if it's a renewable resource.**

coal   plants   oil   ~~sun~~   water   animals

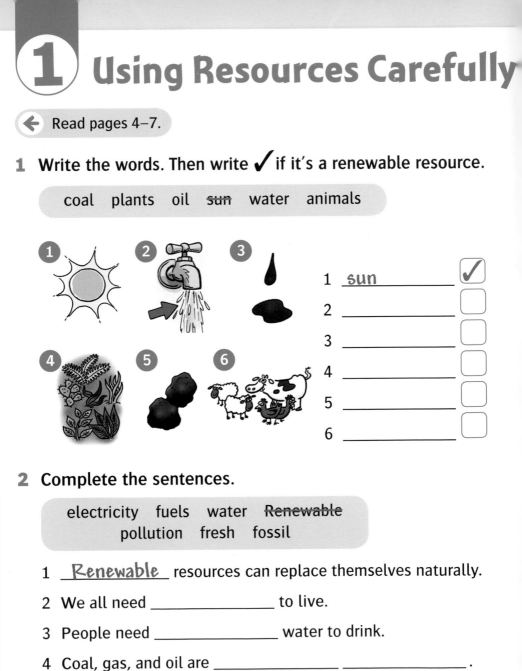

1 ___sun___ ✓

2 _____ ☐

3 _____ ☐

4 _____ ☐

5 _____ ☐

6 _____ ☐

2 **Complete the sentences.**

electricity   fuels   water   ~~Renewable~~
pollution   fresh   fossil

1 ___Renewable___ resources can replace themselves naturally.

2 We all need _____ to live.

3 People need _____ water to drink.

4 Coal, gas, and oil are _____ _____ .

5 We make _____ in power stations.

6 When we make resources dirty this is called _____ .

3 Write five things that use electricity and five things that don't use electricity.

Things that use electricity:

_____

_____

Things that don't use electricity:

_____

_____

4 Answer the questions.

1 What resources can replace themselves naturally?

Renewable resources can replace themselves naturally.

2 Why is water so important?

_____

3 What do people do if there isn't enough water?

_____

4 How can we care for water?

_____

5 What is the problem with fossil fuels?

_____

6 What do you use electricity for?

_____

_____

_____

2 Keeping Our Planet Cool

← Read pages 8–11.

1 Write the numbers.

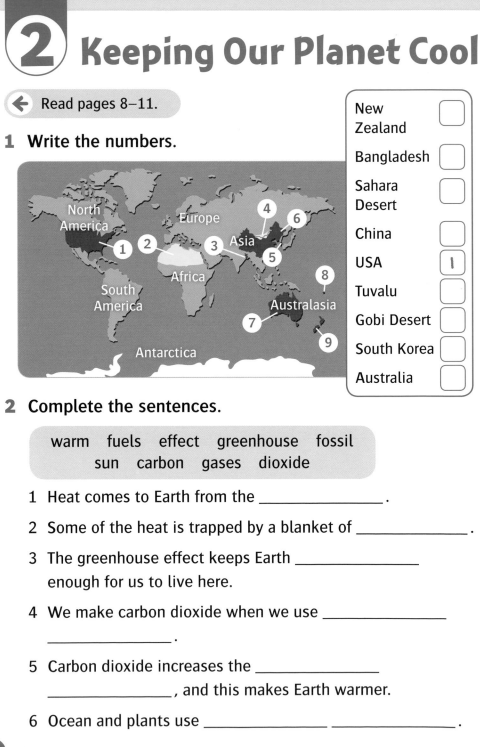

New Zealand ☐

Bangladesh ☐

Sahara Desert ☐

China ☐

USA ☐ |

Tuvalu ☐

Gobi Desert ☐

South Korea ☐

Australia ☐

2 Complete the sentences.

> warm   fuels   effect   greenhouse   fossil
> sun   carbon   gases   dioxide

1 Heat comes to Earth from the _____ .

2 Some of the heat is trapped by a blanket of _____ .

3 The greenhouse effect keeps Earth _____ enough for us to live here.

4 We make carbon dioxide when we use _____ _____ .

5 Carbon dioxide increases the _____ _____ , and this makes Earth warmer.

6 Ocean and plants use _____ _____ .

3 Write *true* or *false*.

1 There are many rivers in Bangladesh. <u>true</u>

2 The Sahara Desert is getting smaller. _____

3 Many people died in a hurricane in New Orleans
in 2005. _____

4 The sea level is getting lower because of
melting ice. _____

5 Funafati is the capital of Tuvalu. _____

6 It's possible to grow food on floating gardens. _____

4 Order the words.

1 increases / Carbon / dioxide / the / effect. / greenhouse

<u>Carbon dioxide increases the greenhouse effect.</u>

2 climate. /global / our / think / is / Scientists / that /
warming / changing

_____

3 10 / level. / Funafati / only / Parts / are / of / centimeters /
sea / above

_____

4 dioxide. / to / has / Our / reduce / natural / planet / ways/
carbon

_____

5 How can we keep our planet cool?

_____

_____

③ Making Clean Electricity

← Read pages 12–15.

1 Complete the diagram.

heat   waves   farms
steam   rivers   sunshine
turbines   tides   panels
colder   sunny   lakes   hot

Geothermal Energy

underground ___heat___

_____ water

_____

Wind Energy

wind _____

wind _____

_____ countries

Energy From Water

_____

_____

ocean _____

ocean _____

Clean Electricity

Solar Energy

_____

solar _____

_____ countries

2 Circle the correct words.

1 Solar energy uses heat from the **sun** / **wind**.

2 Nuclear power stations produce **carbon dioxide** / **radioactive waste**.

3 In Iceland there is lots of hot **wind** / **water** underground.

4 Hydroelectricity is made by using energy from **moving wind** / **water**.

5 The biggest hydroelectric power station is in **France** / **China**.

3 **Correct the sentences.**

1 Nuclear waste is not safe for hundreds of years.

   <u>Nuclear waste is not safe for thousands of years.</u>

2 In Ukraine, 336,000 people had to move to new offices.

   _____

3 We can use solar pools to power watches and calculators.

   _____

4 Wind energy is very useful in hot countries.

   _____

5 Hot wind and steam from underground can heat buildings.

   _____

6 We can make electricity from ocean waste and tides.

   _____

4 **Answer the questions.**

1 Where can we make solar energy easily?

   _____

2 What moving water can we use to make electricity?

   _____

3 How is electricity made in your country?

   _____

   _____

   _____

4 Reducing Travel

← Read pages 16–19.

1 Circle the correct words.

1 We can walk or cycle for **long** / **short** journeys.

2 Small cars use **less** / **more** fuel than big cars.

3 Engineers want to make cars that use **solar energy** / **gasoline**.

4 Catalytic converters change exhaust gases into **cleaner** / **dirtier** gases.

5 Biofuels are made from **fossil fuels** / **plants**.

6 Planes with **bigger** / **smaller** wings use less fuel.

2 Complete the chart.

big cars   catalytic converters   cycling   planes   walking
carbon offsetting   pollution   biofuels   exhaust gases

Good for Earth	Bad for Earth
_____	_____
_____	_____
_____	_____
_____	_____
_____	

3 Complete the puzzle. Write the secret word.

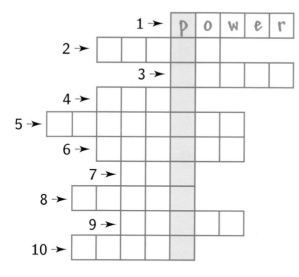

1. We can use electricity to __ cars.
2. If you wash you will be __ .
3. __ energy comes from the sun.
4. They have four wheels and we use them for traveling.
5. These fuels are made from plants.
6. Solar __ don't have much space.
7. This is the opposite of small.
8. For short journeys we can walk or __ .
9. Pollution makes our cities __ .
10. __ use carbon dioxide.

The secret word is:

4 Write about how you travel.

⑤ Keeping Our Planet Clean

← Read pages 20–23.

1 What can we do with our waste? Complete the diagram.

newspapers
garden waste
parts of cars
glass containers
empty cans
food waste
plastic containers
clothes

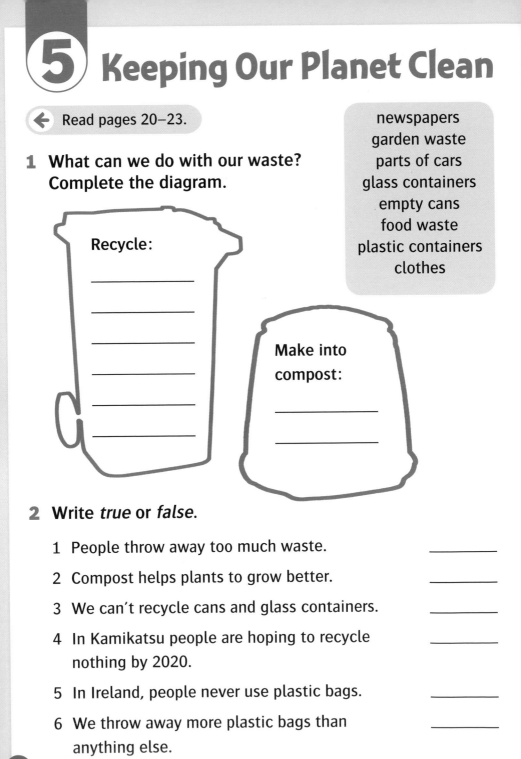

Recycle:

_____
_____
_____
_____
_____
_____

Make into compost:

_____
_____

2 Write *true* or *false*.

1 People throw away too much waste.   _____

2 Compost helps plants to grow better.   _____

3 We can't recycle cans and glass containers.   _____

4 In Kamikatsu people are hoping to recycle nothing by 2020.   _____

5 In Ireland, people never use plastic bags.   _____

6 We throw away more plastic bags than anything else.   _____

3 **Order the words.**

1 animals. / is / for / Pollution / dangerous

_____

2 have / not / people / do / a / water. / About / billion /
clean

_____

3 of / recycle / people / now / lot / a / waste. / Many

_____

4 water. / can / from / factories / Waste / pollute

_____

5 things. / reuse / more / We / try / can / to

_____

4 **Answer the questions.**

1 How is water polluted?

_____

2 How can we change waste into good soil?

_____

3 Why are plastic bags a problem?

_____

4 What things do you reuse?

_____

5 What things do you recycle?

_____

6 Protecting Plants

← Read pages 24–27.

mouse	fox	plant plankton
grass	fish	killer whale
person	sea lion	rabbit	corn
lettuce	owl	cow

1 Complete the food chains.

2 Write true or false.

1 People are at the start of every food chain. _____

2 A rabbit is in the middle of a food chain. _____

3 Plants are important because they give us carbon dioxide. _____

4 We use herbs and spices to make food taste good. _____

5 Plants contain chemicals that can be used as medicines. _____

6 If we use more fossil fuels, we will save millions of plants. _____

3 **Match. Then write the sentences.**

Many useful plants grow	from wheat and corn.
We are using	in rainforests.
Fish	need plants.
We make flour	eat plant plankton.
We all	too many trees.

1 Many useful plants grow in rainforests.

2 _____

3 _____

4 _____

5 _____

4 **Answer the questions.**

1 What do plants need to make their food?

_____

2 What oil is good for your hair and skin?

_____

3 Why do companies cut down trees?

_____

4 How can we protect plants?

_____

_____

Protecting Animals

← Read pages 28–31.

1 Write the animals.

1 kcncieh _____

2 lesif _____

3 nat _____

4 anplehte _____

5 anpda _____

6 cwo _____

7 ebe _____

8 lraogil _____

9 oarpl aebr _____

10 leeebt _____

11 ehspe _____

12 eahwl _____

2 Complete the sentences.

honey   compost   farms   work
animals   eggs   fish   nectar

1 We share our planet with many other _____.

2 Large numbers of fish are raised in _____
_____.

3 Chickens give us _____.

4 Bees get _____ from flowers to
make _____.

5 Animals also help us with _____.

6 Worms help us by making _____.

3 Complete the puzzle.

1 These people kill some animals for money.
2 The special place where an animal lives.
3 If there aren't many of them left, these animals are ___ .
4 This is a huge problem for animals.
5 Birds give us ___ .
6 A very important habitat for animals.
7 A huge animal that lives in the ocean.
8 They give us meat and milk.

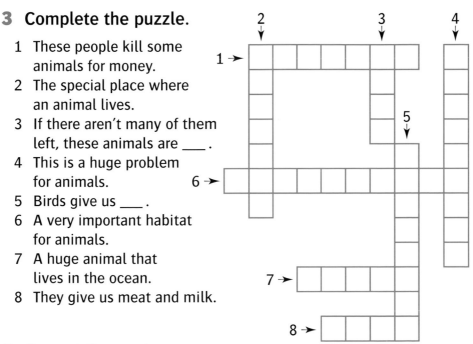

4 Correct the sentences.

1 When we cut down rainforest trees we destroy honey.

_____

2 If the ice at the North Pole grows, polar bears will be in danger.

_____

3 Elephants were hunted because people could sell their tails.

_____

4 Rainforests are the natural habitat of polar bears.

_____

5 Animals are in danger in safari parks.

_____

(8) The Way Forward

← Read pages 32–35.

1 Complete the sentences.

less   reuse   food
energy   electricity
transport   greedy   waste

Problems for our planet:

1 We use too much _____ .

2 We make too much _____ .

3 We _____ food from far away.

How we can care for our planet:

4 We must not be too _____ .

5 We can use _____ energy.

6 We can buy _____ from our own country.

7 We can _____ as much as possible.

8 We can save _____ .

2 Write the opposites. Find the page.

1 protect   _damage_   _____

2 increase   _____   _____

3 old   _____   _____

4 near   _____   _____

5 cold   _____   _____

6 summer   _____   _____

3 **Correct the sentences.**

1   It's important to remember to turn on lights.

_____

2 It's bad to eat fruit from your own country.

_____

3 It's good to reuse and recycle things as little as possible.

_____

4 We cannot help the planet in small ways.

_____

4 **Answer the questions.**

1 Would you like to live in a city or in a village? Why?

_____

_____

2 Where do you buy the food that you eat? Where does it come from?

_____

_____

3 What can we do to care for our planet?

_____

_____

_____

_____

An Animal Poster

1 Imagine you are going to adopt an animal in danger.

2 Write notes and complete the diagram about your animal.

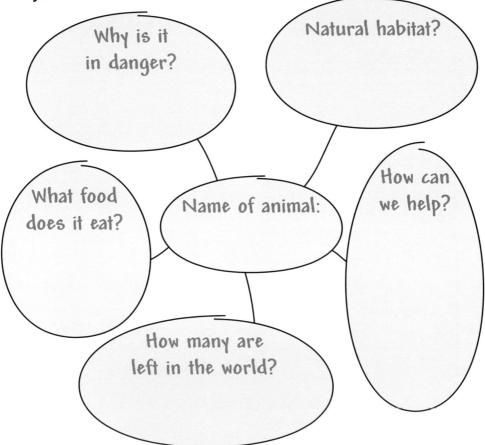

Why is it in danger?

Natural habitat?

What food does it eat?

Name of animal:

How can we help?

How many are left in the world?

3 Make a poster about your animal. Write sentences and add pictures to decorate your poster.

4 Display your poster.

An Electricity Diary

1 Keep an electricity diary. Write ✓ every time you use something that is powered by electricity.

lights	
computer	
television	
CD player	

2 Write about the results. How could you use less electricity?

3 Display your results.

Glossary

Here are some words used in this book, and you can check what they mean. Use a dictionary to check other new words.

accident something that happens by chance

adopt to care for a child or an animal when the parents can't do this

bacteria very simple living things

beetle an insect

blanket a thick cover that you put on a bed

blow to move with the wind

breathe to take in and let out air through your nose and mouth

burn to make flames and heat

cancer a very dangerous disease

capital the main place in a country

carry to take something to another place

change to become different; to make something different

charity (*plural* **charities**) a group of people who collect money to help people or animals

chemical a solid or liquid that is made by chemistry

climate the usual type of weather in a country

coal a hard, black fuel

comfortable nice to be in, for example, soft beds or chairs

company a group of people that makes money by producing or selling things

contain to have something inside

countryside the land outside a town or city

cover to put something over something; to be over something

crop a plant that we grow in large amounts

dam a structure that is built across a river to catch the water

damage to make something bad or weak

decompose to break down into smaller parts

destroy to damage something very badly

die to stop living

divide to break something into smaller parts

energy we need energy to move and grow, and machines need energy to work

engine a machine that produces energy to move a vehicle

enough how much we want or need

escape to get away from something

everyday normal, not special

exercise what we do when we move to stay healthy

exhaust gases bad air that comes out of the back of a car

extreme very strong and dangerous

feathers the soft parts that cover a bird's body

float to stay on the top of water

fly (*plural* **flies**) an insect

forest a place with a lot of trees

fresh clean and cool

fuel something that we use to produce heat or energy

furniture tables, chairs, beds, etc.

gas it's not a solid or a liquid; like air

gasoline (*or* **petrol**) a liquid that burns and powers an engine

glass a hard material; you can make bottles and windows with it

greedy wanting more than you need

greenhouse a building made of glass for growing plants

grow to get bigger

healthy not sick

huge very big

human from people

hurricane a very strong wind

increase to get bigger, or to make something bigger

insect a very small animal with six legs

investigate to find out about something

island land with water all around

isolated far from other places

ivory tusks the white teeth of elephants

kill to make something or someone die

lake a big area of water

leather the skin of an animal; we use it to make shoes and jackets

light bulb the glass part of an electric lamp that produces light

main the biggest or most important

material something that we use to make other things

medicine something that you take when you are sick, to make you better

melt to change into a liquid, like water

minibeast a very small animal

modern of today; not from the past

natural from nature; not made by people

natural resources something produced by our planet, that we can use

nectar a sweet liquid produced by flowers

nuclear energy energy that is made by breaking or joining atoms

oil a liquid from plants or animals that we use for cooking or to make gasoline

oxygen a gas that we need to breathe

palm oil a thick liquid from palm trees

passenger someone who travels in a bus, train, plane, ship, for example

planet a large, round thing in space that goes around a star

plastic a man-made material

pollen the yellow powder in flowers

pollute to make land, water, or air dirty

power to make something work or operate

power station a building where electricity is made

predict to say what will happen in the future

problem something that isn't easy

produce to grow or make something

protect to keep safe from danger

public transportation vehicles that we can share like buses, planes, trains

raise to feed and take care of animals

rare not very many; not very often

recycle to use again; to make something new

reduce to make something smaller or less

replace to put a new thing back in the place of an old one

reuse to use again

river water on land that goes to the ocean

road sign a thing near a road with words or pictures on it to tell you what to do

run out when there is no more of something

sea level how high the water is in the sea or ocean

sheep (*plural* **sheep**) an animal that we raise for wool and meat

ship a big boat

similar like someone or something

soil the ground that plants grow in

solar from the sun

space an area where there is nothing; where the moon and stars are

special different from what is normal

steam the hot gas that water makes when it boils

store to keep something to use later

technology the design of new things

temperature how hot or cold something is

tide the movement of the ocean toward land and away from land

tiny very small

transport to take something or someone from one place to another in a vehicle

trap to keep something in a place where it can't escape

treat to make a sick person well again

useful that helps someone to do something

vehicle something that transports goods or people

village a group of houses together in the countryside; it's smaller than a town

vitamin something in food that makes us healthy; they are called A, B, C, etc.

waste to use something more than you have to; things that we throw away

water wheel a wheel that turns in moving water to make energy

wave a line of water that moves across the top of the ocean

wing birds and planes have wings to help them to fly

without not having something; not doing something

wool the soft, thick hair of sheep

worm a long, thin animal with no legs

Oxford Read and Discover

Series Editor: Hazel Geatches • CLIL Adviser: John Clegg

Oxford Read and Discover graded readers are at six levels, for students from age 6 and older. They cover many topics within three subject areas, and support English across the curriculum, or Content and Language Integrated Learning (CLIL).

Available for each reader:
- Audio CD Pack (book & audio CD)
- Activity Book

Teaching notes & CLIL guidance: **www.oup.com/elt/teacher/readanddiscover**

Subject Area / Level	The World of Science & Technology	The Natural World	The World of Arts & Social Studies
1 300 headwords	• Eyes • Fruit • Trees • Wheels	• At the Beach • Camouflage • In the Sky • Young Animals	• Art • Schools
2 450 headwords	• Electricity • Plastic • Sunny and Rainy • Your Body	• Earth • Farms • In the Mountains • Wild Cats	• Cities • Jobs
3 600 headwords	• How We Make Products • Sound and Music • Super Structures • Your Five Senses	• Amazing Minibeasts • Animals in the Air • Life in Rainforests • Wonderful Water	• Festivals Around the World • Free Time Around the World
4 750 headwords	• All About Plants • How to Stay Healthy • Machines Then and Now • Why We Recycle	• All About Desert Life • All About Ocean Life • Animals at Night • Incredible Earth	• Animals in Art • Wonders of the Past
5 900 headwords	• Materials to Products • Medicine Then and Now • Transportation Then and Now • Wild Weather	• All About Islands • Animal Life Cycles • Exploring Our World • Great Migrations	• Homes Around the World • Our World in Art
6 1,500 headwords	• Cells and Microbes • Clothes Then and Now • Incredible Energy • Your Amazing Body	• All About Space • Caring for Our Planet • Earth Then and Now • Wonderful Ecosystems	• Food Around the World • Helping Around the World

Readers in GRAY available 2013